IMAGES
of America

ALONG
THE KENNEBEC
THE HERMAN BRYANT COLLECTION

There is much we will never know about this extraordinary man and the time in which he lived. But if pictures are worth the proverbial thousand words, perhaps you will come to know this artist and this period of our history for yourself. You too will feel you were there a century ago, along the Kennebec River.

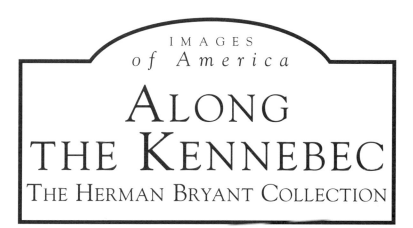

IMAGES
of America

ALONG
THE KENNEBEC
THE HERMAN BRYANT COLLECTION

Gay M. Grant

ARCADIA

First published 1995
Copyright © Gay M. Grant, 1995

ISBN 0-7524-0251-X

Published by Arcadia Publishing,
an imprint of the Chalford Publishing Corporation,
One Washington Center, Dover, New Hampshire 03820.
Printed in Great Britain

Library of Congress Cataloging-in-Publication Data applied for

This book is dedicated to the memory of
Pauline (Polly) Verna Nute (1905–1995),
a lifelong resident of South Gardiner village.

Polly was my next door neighbor, my mentor, and my friend.
She entrusted me with the Herman Bryant Collection,
and with her own stories.
One day, as we sat in her front room watching the river flow by, Polly said,
"Father Time is a relentless fellow. One day he will knock on your door."
The memories and images of our collective past are our heritage.
When I struggled with how to put all of this material together, she said,
"it will come together in due time." I only wish it had come a little sooner.
Polly's death in March brought it all home to me. "Tell the stories," she said.
This book represents twelve years of research and a friendship.

Polly is with me still.

Contents

Acknowledgments

Many people gave their time, assistance, and support very generously during the creation of this book. It would be impossible to mention everyone here, but I would like to thank the following: Bruce Johnson, Wallace Atkins, Roy Bailey, Ethel Ladner, Horace Hildreth, Lawrence Caney, Mrs. Caroline Noble, Richard D. and Arnold Noble Weeks, Ellen and Charles Annis, Mrs. E.D., Donald White, and of course, Polly.

I would also like to acknowledge the help of: Robert Belgrade, the late Linwood "Gus" Westerlund, James Connor, Rinaldo Colby, Jody Clark, Noreen Cop, Jean Hall, Anne Beattie, Rob Saucier, Imogene Caney Fair, Greg Hart and Brian Sipe of the Maine State Museum, Roy Wells of the Maine State Archives, and Karen and Crosby Milliman at the Colburn House Museum.

On a more personal note, others who contributed their support were: my sister, Bonny Myshrall Saxon; my friends, Cathy Sears, Jan Brackett, and Jeff, Deb, and Andrew Temple; my children, Aaron and Melody; Arlen Finseth; my grandparents, Keith and Thelma Condon Harriman; and my husband, editor, and best friend, Ron Grant.

Some of the inspiration that prompted me to work on this history came from: Gardiner's Jane Morrison (1947–1987), a talented film maker who inspired me with her work on the life of Sarah Orne Jewett, *Master Smart Woman*. Jane was a friend of Polly's and borrowed from the Herman Bryant Collection for that work. Another great inspiration to me was Lew Dietz' collection of Kosti Ruohomaa's photographs *Night Train At Wisasset Station*, which was given to me by my mother, Sylvia Harriman Myshrall.

Introduction

This is not just a wonderful collection of old photographs. What you hold in your hands represents a man's life. This realization came to me only recently, though I have been the caretaker of Herman Bryant's photographic work for over twelve years. The blurry figure of the artist himself has finally cleared in my focus and I feel as though I know a man who died in 1937—twenty-three years before I was born.

In my mind's eye, I can see him waiting on the bank of the Kennebec River. There is his camera on its tripod. Under the black cloth he waits for the steamship to pass behind the island before he squeezes the trigger, freezing its image on a piece of emulsion-coated glass. Through listening to those who knew him, a character has finally come to life. In his pictures I can feel his love for his only child, Minnie, and for his beloved wife, Viola. Herman's nephew, Frank Bryant, lived his childhood in his uncle's care and the myriad photographs of him are testament to the affection Herman had for his brother's son. Bryant's sense of humor, his love of children and animals, his home and garden, and his community are there in his compositions. When I read a news clipping noting that in 1929 his hand was crushed in a gravel loader, I felt sadness, as if for a friend.

Herman Bryant was born in 1858 in Hartland, Vermont. As a young man he came to Gardiner, then an emerging industrial community ideally situated along the western bank of the Kennebec River. Like so many others he came in search of work and to be with a young woman he wished to marry. He married his sweetheart, Viola English, they built a simple home on a hill overlooking the river in South Gardiner, and Herman went to work in the Lawrence Lumber Mill. Viola worked in their home and they had their daughter and then later a nephew to raise. They planted a garden and an orchard. Herman was clerk of the South Gardiner Volunteer Fire Company and recorded its meetings faithfully until the month before his death. Together with their friends and neighbors, the Thurlows, the Bryants owned a small motor boat (the *Minnie and Mary*, named for the eldest child of each family), and a coastal cottage. The Bryants lived what was then only emerging as the "American Dream." Except for the fact that Herman chronicled every aspect of their lives with his camera, theirs was a very ordinary, turn-of-the-century family life.

When my husband and I moved into my childhood home in South Gardiner, the ink was not yet dry on my history degree certificate and my longtime friend Polly said, "we have to do the history of South Gardiner, I have to do something with these pictures." She and Angie Dutton, another Bryant family friend, took care of Miss Minnie Bryant in her old age. When Miss Bryant had said to Polly, "You take Dad's pictures," Polly assumed she meant the scattering of old family albums.

In 1980, Minnie died and the house was to be torn down. The gravel below the house was worth more than the house itself and was sold to the city. In the house, Polly found box after box of glass plates in crumbling yellowed envelopes, some marked in Herman's neat hand, many blank. Polly seemed to know that she would not live long enough to see to their disposition herself, so she gave them into my safekeeping.

I knew that we had to get them into safe archival storage before they were lost forever. For over twelve years I cataloged them for the Maine State Museum, where they will belong to the people of Maine. All told there are 781 glass plates, 332 photographs, and innumerable albums and postcards. There are Bryant family photographs, and photographs of people, homes, farms, mills, public buildings, the railroad, shipping, and ice harvesting. The backdrop or subject in so many of these photographs is the Kennebec River—the gateway from central Maine to the Atlantic Ocean. To preserve Bryant's style, I have retained his photograph titles where they exist. His titles are set at the beginning of the captions, with quotation marks around them.

Captured in time by the lens of an amateur photographer, these images shed light on a past we can otherwise only read about. What is written is never as powerful as that we see for ourselves. In his *History of Photography*, Beaumont Newhall writes: "The fundamental belief in the authenticity of photographs explains why photographs of people no longer living and of vanished architecture are so melancholy. Neither words nor yet the most detailed painting can evoke a moment of vanished time so powerfully and so completely as a good photograph."

Newhall goes on to say that it was these amateur photographers who, through experimentation with subjects, lighting, chemicals, and equipment, dominated the field and pushed the boundaries of this new art form. Bryant's only exhibition in his lifetime was in the form of the postcards he had printed and the family photographs he took for his neighbors and friends. He was a quiet man. Even those who knew him were surprised at the number of images he left behind as a treasure for us to discover.

The pictures themselves are powerful enough. Yet I discovered that another treasure came in the stories they evoked in those older people we shared them with. Memories surfaced. There was laughter and sadness. There were the unprintable stories you will have to imagine! Through the pages of this book you can be there with me, listening as reminiscence dispelled time. Oral history illuminates everyday life in a way that no other source can. Polly's many stories appear here, as well as anecdotes from other South Gardiner residents: Ethel Ladner, Roy Bailey, Bruce Johnson, Wallace ("Wally") Atkins, Don White, and Arnold Noble Weeks. Perhaps these anecdotes and photographs will stimulate your own memories, or inspire you to listen to an older relative or neighbor. Time does not stand still. Several of the people I spoke with are no longer living. Listen while you can.

One
Families
and Children

The Herman Bryant Collection offers a glimpse into the daily life of an ordinary family in rural Maine at the turn of the century. Bryant's images and the valuable nuggets of information that have been gleaned from oral history speak of simpler lives. As is so often the case with the telling of history, however, the reality may well have been different from the way it appears in photographs or the way it is remembered, but both views of history can be appreciated in the images and words collected here.

At the turn of the century lives centered on home, church, and community. Families—including children—worked together to make a living in what could be a very harsh environment. In some ways Bryant was an idealist, and certainly a romantic: his photographs portray an ideal vision of childhood and family life, or perhaps quite simply he deliberately recorded life in its better moments. Whatever his intention was, the combination of these photographs and local reminiscences is a surprisingly complete picture of life in rural Maine as the nineteenth century gave way to an almost unthinkably different twenty-first.

Twins, possibly Bryant's nieces, in a rocker, c. 1900.

The Bryant family in their backyard, *c.* 1905. The Bryants had one child, Minnie. Bryant's nephew Frank ("Frankie") Bryant also lived in their home for most of his childhood. Maine backyards still sport tents and hammocks during the brief summer.

"Group Gravel Bank," *c.* 1900. Herman, Frankie, Viola, and Minnie sit by the gravel bank behind their house. The Bryant home sat nestled beside a hill on Phillips Street in South Gardiner, on the other side of which was a gravel pit. Over the years, Bryant took many panoramic photographs of the Kennebec River from this hill.

"Viola and Minnie," August 14, 1898. Viola J. English Bryant (1854–1936) and her daughter, Minnie Bryant (1886–1980), in the Bryant parlor. The shelf above the settee holds family bric-a-brac and Bryant portraits and landscapes—pictures cleverly captured within the picture.

Minnie Bryant *c.* 1902. The Herman Bryant Collection is replete with photographs of the Bryants' only child at every stage of her life and in her many lovely outfits—all of which were sewn by her mother. She was a patient model and only occasionally showed expressions of boredom. Here she is about sixteen years old, perhaps wearing her hair "up" for the first time.

"Frankie and Black Kitty," *c.* 1900. Frank Bryant was the son of Herman's brother. After his mother died, the Bryants went to Vermont to bring the little boy to stay for a while. He stayed.

"English Group," *c.* 1898. This is Viola's family, the English family. Herman is in the back row, first from the left; Minnie is in the back row, second from the right; Viola is in the second row, first from the left; and Frankie is the little one in the sailor suit. The old man with the white beard in the center of the photograph is also seen in other photographs that are simply labelled "Grandpa."

"My Room," *c.* 1903. Minnie's bedroom, a typical teenager's room complete with the posters and decorations that were fashionable at the time. Her mother was thirty-two and her father twenty-six when she was born, and—perhaps because she was essentially an only child—she was always the "apple of their eye." This remained her room until she went into a nursing home shortly before her death at the age of ninety-four.

"Minnie and Cabin," January 30, 1903. How many generations of American schoolchildren have built "log" cabins for school projects?

"Minnie and Roses," *c.* 1910.

"Minnie's dolls," *c.* 1902. The calendar on the wall says January 1902.

"Frankie at Old Orchard," c. 1900. Ethel Ladner's most lasting memory of Frankie is that "he was freckle faced and had red hair."

"Frank and tools," c. 1905. Plumbing systems were still fairly basic at the turn of the century. A.N. Weeks (1896–1988), a former neighbor of the Bryant family, explains a fairly typical homemade system: "Our water supply was a cistern dug below the cellar floor into which the rainwater from the roof was piped. . . . The water was lifted to the kitchen sink by a hand operated pitcher pump." After her parents died, Minnie kept the family home true to the memories of the days when they lived there with her.

16

"Gathering Sap," c. 1905. Frank was one member of the family whose life did not continue the simple, almost pastoral, pattern begun in his childhood. It affected Minnie very deeply, as Polly remembers: "You know, the last of Miss Bryant's living . . . she kept wondering what happened to Frank. She'd like to know. She didn't know. He kind of went wild."

"Frank with Violin," c. 1915. Don White echoes Polly's observations: "During World War I, he claimed that he was in the army. Well he wasn't. He had a uniform on and was getting out of it, see. . . . The military came and picked him up . . . no one ever knew where he went to."

"Minnie, Elmer, and Chickens," *c.* 1902. Most nineteenth-century Maine households were fairly self-sufficient and the Bryant household was no different. Don White has a particular memory about the Bryants' hen house: "The old hen house sat back of the house. I can remember when Mr. Bryant built that. He had just fixed the concrete floor and my brother—he was just a small kid—he walked in that and so far as I know his tracks, bare footed, were always there! Mr. Bryant didn't say anything. He was a man that would never raise his voice."

Frank fishing at the creek, *c.* 1900.

"Frank," *c.* 1915. Growing up in the days when neighbors thought that it was acceptable to know everything about each other means that Don White remembers all kinds of details about life with the Bryants, including a vague memory of this bicycle: "Frank's bicycle! Now that was really something. The only one I ever saw with a wheel instead of handle bars. Herman Bryant bought it. I never forgot seeing that!"

"Falls, Minnie and Frankie," November 17, 1907. One of many streams which flow into the Kennebec River, this "crick" flows over Lawrence Falls, under the River Road (Route 24), and under an adjacent railroad trestle to the Kennebec River.

"Group Six Young Ladies," September 5, 1914. Minnie (at the far left) and five of her girlfriends at the Bryant home. This photograph may have been taken on the day they graduated from high school.

"Viola, Minnie and Rock," October 2, 1898. Mrs. Bryant was remembered fondly by Minnie's young friends. Don White has a particularly childlike memory: "Mrs. Bryant? She was nice. Every time we went over there she always had a cookie!"

This photograph, taken on the riverbank across from the Congregational Church *c.* 1920, includes Ernestine Alexander (at the far left), Helen Larrabee (second from the left), and Pauline Nute (fifth from the left). Polly remembers that in the sedate town of Gardiner the young people found entertainment where they could. "We used to take a walk every Sunday afternoon. We didn't have anything else to do. We'd end up down to Hamlin's big kitchen and we'd wait down there until we went to Youth Group . . . we called ourselves the "Christian Endeavors." Polly later served as minister of this church.

"Mr. Thurlow's House," c. 1900. Walter Thurlow was a carpenter and builder in Gardiner. The Thurlows were neighbors and friends of the Bryants and the two families shared a boat and a summer cottage.

"Mrs. Thurlow, Marjorie and Mary," c. 1900.

"Mary Thurlow," c. 1898. Little Mary Thurlow sitting with her toy and cat on the front steps of the Thurlow farm on a winter's day. The boat that the Bryants and Thurlows owned together was named the *Minnie and Mary* after the two eldest daughters of the families.

"School Children," *c*. 1900.

Little girl with piano.

"Stewart Children," c. 1900. The Stewart family, which included two children of Minnie's generation—Ruby and a younger brother—lived at the top of Sherburn Avenue.

"Elsie Munson," July 4, 1902. This local girl is dressed up for Fourth of July festivities.

"Gertrude Lawrence," *c*. 1900. Gertrude, the fifth child of Charles Lawrence, Jr., was born in 1897. She died of appendicitis at the tender age of six on October 20, 1903.

"Harold Erskine," *c*. 1900. Harold was the nephew of Mrs. Wallace Lawrence (formerly Alice Erskine). Wallace and Alice Lawrence had no children of their own.

"Crosby Children," *c.* 1900. A little girl's doll was her most prized possession.

Father and children, *c.* 1900.

"Beard Twins," December 24, 1903. Bryant seemed to enjoy photographing children more than any other subject. Perhaps it was their simplicity and unpredictability that charmed him. These children, contemporaries of Minnie, lived nearby.

"Mrs. Hildreth and Babies," February 22, 1903. Florence Townley Lawrence Hildreth holding her twin sons, Horace and Charles. Their father died when the boys were young and Mrs. Hildreth later married Dr. R.D. Simons and moved the family to Gardiner. Both boys were remembered as football stars in a town that loved its sports. Horace Hildreth went on to serve as governor of Maine from 1945 to 1949.

"Tree and Children—Erskine," c. 1903. Christmas was special to Bryant and he longed for a family Christmas like this even before he was married. He wrote to Viola from Hartland, Vermont, on December 25, 1880: "You wanted me to write you when I would be there . . . you may look for me next Friday. . . . I am getting pretty lonesome and want to get back. I hope you had a pleasant Christmas and some of that Turkey."

"Willey family," July 30, 1899. Fred Willey and his wife, Fannie Foster Crocker, with their children. They built this house just behind the railroad station in South Gardiner. The house later belonged to Roy Bailey. It still has the letters carved above the window frames.

This is Don White as an infant. Don still lives in the area, and the occasions of some of these pictures are as fresh in his mind as the day they were taken. "I lived across the street from the Bryants when I was small. I can remember that picture down at the house."

"Linwood Eastman," *c.* 1910. Throughout the centuries, sleds have meant hours of fun for children during the long, cold Maine winters. The Eastmans lived near the Bryants in a house overlooking the Kennebec River. Linwood (1895–1963) worked in the Lawrence Mill until it closed, and also served in World War I.

Two

People At Home

Owning a home was the hope of most families at the turn of the century and South Gardiner had land affordable to working people. The carefully tended buildings and gardens, from the Gardiner Mansion to the simplest dwelling, are testimony to the great pride that was felt by the owners of even the most basic homes.

As photography became more widespread in the late nineteenth century, families of modest means could afford to have portraits made or special occasions recorded on film. Despite the instant popularity of photography, however, the Herman Bryant Collection remains special because it gives us an intimate glimpse into the everyday life of one family in an era when most photographs were quite formal. The collection therefore contains an eclectic mixture of informal snaps and commissioned family portraits, which when examined side by side, emphasize the vast differences between the two "genres."

"Looking Down River From Hill," c. 1900. This photograph shows Viola and Minnie in their garden. The hill from which Bryant took his panoramic views of the Kennebec is now a gaping hole in the earth—the city gravel pit. The Bryant home was torn down when it was realized that the gravel beneath it had become more valuable than the house itself.

"Viola and Herman," c. 1880. Viola and Herman Bryant were obviously very much in love and yearning to be together in the 1880s. This is an extract from a letter from Herman in Hartland, Vermont, to Viola in South Gardiner, Maine, dated November 7, 1880.

"Viola,

I am glad that you like [it] so well there. I should think it would be very pleasant there by the river-side. You wrote that you thought you could have a place in a shoe shop at Richmond and sent me the overseer's address thinking I would like to get a chance there. I should like to very much for it would be so pleasant if we could be together there: it don't seem as though I could stay up here all winter and not see you. . . .

From one who thinks of you, Herman."

"Saturday Night," c. 1903. At the turn of the century it was normal to work twelve hours a day, six days a week. Saturday night was therefore a very special evening, when the working people took their baths and put on their "Sunday clothes" for an evening out—perhaps a dance or play at the local hall—before church the next morning.

"Viola, Frank, and Analdo," *c.* 1910. Viola's brother, Analdo English, was also an amateur photographer. At this time, taking and developing photographs was still very much in the experimental stage, but it is recognized throughout the photography world that it was amateurs like Bryant and English that were responsible for pushing the frontiers of this new technology.

"Doctor Sawyer House," December 28, 1899. This house was beside the Highland Avenue Methodist Church in Gardiner.

"Parlor, Doctor Sawyer," December 28, 1899. Minnie and Viola Bryant with Mrs. Sawyer. A portrait of the late doctor can also be seen in the photograph.

"Fogg House," December 25, 1898. This house was next to the Bryants'. It was later converted to serve as a garage for Minnie Bryant's car.

"Mr. and Mrs. Fogg," *c*. 1900.

"Clarence Beedles Family," December 22, 1901. George Clarence Beedle (1848–1931), married Annie L. Richardson (1858–1950) in 1879. They had three children: Laurie, Louise, and George. This photograph shows the family with a son-in-law and some grandchildren in the parlor.

"Beedle House," c. 1900. This house on the River Road belonged to the Clarence Beedle family. It is now owned by Warren and Millie Gay.

The original David Lawrence homestead on Delong's Hill in South Gardiner, *c.* 1875. The Lawrence family was the driving force of the village of South Gardiner, to the extent that the railroad referred to the area as "Lawrence Mills."

David Lawrence came to the area from Littleton, Massachusetts, in 1769. He and his wife, Sarah Eastman Lawrence, settled on a tract of land purchased from Thomas Hancock, a Kennebec Proprietor who traced his ownership to the original Plymouth Land Grant. Creating their wealth by cutting timber to send downriver for shipbuilding, the Lawrence family typified the American pioneering and entrepreneurial spirit. David served in the Revolutionary War and marched with Benedict Arnold to Quebec. He was widowed three times, had fourteen children, and left his fourth wife a widow in 1836. (Courtesy of Imogene Caney Fair.)

The Charles Lawrence, Sr. house, with Charles Lawrence, Jr. (by the horse), Coburn Lawrence (on the bicycle), Florence Lawrence, the first Mrs. Lawrence, and a friend. The house (located just north of the David Lawrence homestead shown on page 38) was razed by a fire on March 12, 1883. All that remained after the conflagration were the barns: the house, ell, and shed were all destroyed and the occupants were lucky to escape with what clothes they could throw on. A few articles of furniture were saved, but the late Charles Lawrence, Sr.'s papers were lost. He had died only a few days before, on March 4, 1883. (Courtesy of Imogene Caney Fair.)

The Charles Lawrence, Jr. house, c. 1890. Charles Lawrence, Jr. built a home on the site of his late father's house. This photograph shows his second wife May Lawrence (on the left), their daughter Madelon on the arm of the chair, Agnes the hired girl (on the right), and Shep the dog. This house was also badly damaged by fire in 1891 and around 1920 it burned to the ground. A small bungalow built by Earle Dutton sits on this site today. (Courtesy of Imogene Caney Fair.)

"Cope Lawrence and Dog," April 7, 1899. Coburn Lawrence (1876–1943) was the only son of Charles Lawrence, Jr. Local people remember that "Cope" was responsible for checking lumber when the cars were loaded, and that he was a musician.

"Lawrence Group," August 27, 1899. The Lawrences on the front lawn of Sherburn Lawrence's house on Main Street (later called Riverview Drive) with the Kennebec River behind them. The home now belongs to Brian and Nancy Rines.

"Harry Lawrence House," c. 1900. This house later belonged to Wallace Lawrence. It is now owned by the Farnsworth family.

"Hiram Lawrence," January 1906. Hiram Lawrence (1829–1906) is shown here with his nurse on the front porch of his house on Main Street. His obituary in the *Kennebec Journal* on October 24, 1906, read: "Mr. Lawrence was a man of quiet, domestic tastes, and by his kind and unassuming ways, greatly endeared himself to all who knew him. He was a great sufferer during many years of his life, passing through many illnesses, a year ago suffering from a trouble which necessitated the amputation of his right leg. All these things he endured with exemplary patience and gentleness . . ."

"Nine Am, Light Clouds," August 31, 1902. The Sherburn Lawrence house on Main Street in South Gardiner. Sherburn Lawrence was the eldest son of Charles Lawrence, Sr. and one of the five partners (all Lawrence siblings) of the Lawrence Mill. Sherburn and his wife, Julia Stanford, had one son, Forrest, who died in 1888 at the age of thirty-two. This photograph shows Forrest Lawrence's widow, Mrs. Abbie Willey Lawrence, and their son, Perley M. Lawrence together with Mrs. Julia Lawrence.

"Abbie's Store," c. 1902. As in many New England mill towns, the lives of the mill workers and the development of the surrounding community were very much bound up with the mill, which often supplied local services. "Forrest Hall" was built by Forrest Lawrence next door to the Sherburn Lawrence house and directly opposite the Lawrence Mills in 1881. It replaced the small general store that had become the mill office and it served a variety of purposes. It contained an apartment for Forrest, his wife Abbie, and their young son, as well as the post office and a huge meeting hall upstairs. Abbie Willey Lawrence continued the dry goods store and post office after her husband's death. According to the obituary in the local paper, at the age of forty-seven she became "despondent" after a long illness and the amputation of a leg, and took an overdose of strychnine which killed her. For a time the building was Walter Preble's general store. It was torn down around 1910.

"Flowers, Abbie Lawrence," 1904. The obituary in the *Gardiner Reporter Journal* noted that Abbie Willey Lawrence was "very well and favorably known in South Gardiner . . . survived by one son Perley, a student at Kent's Hill."

"Hiram Bachelder and Engine," *c.* 1900. This photograph shows the interior of the Lawrence Mill at the turn of the century. The mill still features in the memories of local people, such as Bruce Johnson, who remembers that it was "powered by burning slab wood and log ends."

"H. Bachelder and Mrs.," December 1908. Hiram L. Bachelder (1851–1910) and his wife, Emma F. Bachelder (1853–1914), in the parlor of their home on Sawyer Street in South Gardiner.

"Hiram Bachelder's House," *c.* 1908.

"Bachelder Flowers," 1910. The Bachelders had two children, a son and daughter, but neither survived infancy.

"Tarbox House," *c*. 1890. This is probably Wallace Tarbox (1850–1930), the only child of James and Dolly Lawrence Tarbox, and his wife, Clara C. Mayville Tarbox (1851–1923), outside their house by the "mountain." Today the "mountain" is covered with pines, and the house is owned by the Potter family.

"Mayhew Group," *c*. 1900. This portrait shows the Mayhew family at their house on Phillips Street, close to the Bryant house. According to a report in the July 27, 1900, edition of the *Daily Reporter Journal*, "the price of real estate in South Gardiner is reasonable and the poor laboring man can afford to build."

46

"H. Goodin House," c. 1900. This house, on Sherburn Avenue in South Gardiner, was typical of many Gardiner homes, with a front porch from which one could watch the world go by.

"Libby House," c. 1910. This house, on Bartlett Street in South Gardiner, was decorated with gingerbread trim. No doubt the boys on the porch would rather be sledding than putting the firewood in! The house later burned to the ground.

"Dennis Pitts, Horses," c. 1900. This house on the Capen Road is a classic New England farmhouse. It is owned today by the Gregoire family. In the winter Mainers would travel by horse and sled, and such driving was always preferred to the arduous travel through the mud of spring or the dust of summer.

"Maggie P. and Vera Bryant," November 1909. These young women seem ready to take on the world, yet there were few options open to women at this time. Few rural women with little or no means attended college. Polly remembers being one of the least well-off girls at Gordon College in Massachusetts. "I had two dresses, one I wore every day in the week, every night I was either washing it or sponging it here and there so it wouldn't smell, and I wore that a whole semester. . . . Not many went to school with any less clothes than I had . . . I couldn't have gone if I hadn't gone that way."

Three
People At Work

The images in the Herman Bryant Collection were taken during the Kennebec River region's industrial heyday, when mills, shops, ice houses, and shipyards lined the banks of the river. Gardiner was ideally situated at the point where deep water navigation became possible and the Cobbosseecontee and other streams provided abundant water power to fuel the mills.

Its location on the banks of the powerful Kennebec allowed the Gardiner area to develop into a regional industrial center in the nineteenth century. The region had some of the most modern paper mills in the country as well as lumber mills; box, toy, and furniture factories; ice houses; shipyards; and blacksmithing and carpentry shops. These and other industries supported a young population that grew steadily throughout the Victorian era.

Changing technology and the depletion of the area's natural resources brought prosperity to a halt. With the dawn of the twentieth century, the mills burned or became obsolete and were closed down. The Kennebec River, once known for the purity of its ice, was almost dead by the 1960s and had become virtually an open sewage system. Environmental laws and treatment plants have fortunately returned much of the river's life, though it is still far from pristine. Today its recreational and scenic possibilities are again being developed, and people are once again optimistic.

"Dummy Train," c. 1900. This train carried workers from South Gardiner to the mills in Augusta.

"Rail Road Station, South Gardiner, Maine," c. 1900. The railroad was for years an integral part of the smooth operation of industries in the Gardiner area. As South Gardiner resident Bruce Johnson remembers: "For years when we got on a train in Gardiner and paid our fare we got a slip, and it was punched with every town that was on the Maine Central. They'd punch us on at Gardiner and off at 'Lawrence Mills.' That was before 1920."

"MCRR Yard SG: Snow View From Bridge," February 14, 1899. Clearing snow from the Maine Central Railroad's turning house and tracks. This bridge, known locally as "Minnie's Bridge," spanned the railroad tracks and connected Main (Riverview Drive was called "Main Street" until Route 24 was constructed in 1934) and Phillips Streets.

50

"Building Bridge," January 23, 1898. Railroad bridges like this one carry trains across the many tributary streams along the west side of the Kennebec River. At this time twenty-six passenger trains ran to Augusta per day. An express train to Boston took five-and-a-half hours

"RR Station Gardiner, Old," April 1911. This wooden station was built in 1851. It was replaced in 1911 by a grand structure that still graces the center of town, so we can presume that Bryant took this photograph to create an historic record of the old station. South Gardiner students who attended high school in Gardiner had to rush to the station each morning to catch the train. Polly remembers the schedule well: "At 6:25 . . . I used to race the train down the hill. I'd eat my breakfast. I'd be watching and eating. When the "Scoot" got just a certain place I'd grab the book and run down the hill. They'd toot the horn!"

"Wrecked Car," September 2, 1905. Bryant was on hand with his camera to record one of the state's worst railroad accidents. At 3:15 a.m. on September 2, 1905, Train 127, the eastbound express to Bar Harbor, smashed into another train waiting at South Gardiner Station. Many passengers were seriously hurt, and a special train brought doctors from Gardiner to assist Dr. Libby and nurse Elizabeth Craig, who were the first on the scene. According to the September 3, 1905, edition of the *Kennebec Journal*, the official cause of the accident was fog: because the "brakeman" was obscured from view, the engine of the second train "plowed its way clean into the rear coach [of the first train] and lifted it high into the air, to fall again with its shrieking and terror stricken passengers, fighting their way through windows to air and freedom." A special "wrecking train" was sent down from Waterville and the area was cleared in time for the arrival of the next train in two hours.

"Wrecked Car View Two," September 2, 1905.

"Where Wreck Occurred," September 2, 1905.

"Ice Harvesting," December 1905. Before every home and business had a refrigerator, ice was harvested from frozen rivers each winter and stored in sawdust in huge ice houses until the spring. Ice cut from the Kennebec River was known for its purity and Gardiner was the center of this major industry. Ice harvesting from bodies of water all over Maine provided winter work for local people (particularly farmers) as well as for an influx of transient workers who came from as far away as Aroostook County to find work in the bleak Maine winters.

This photograph shows work at the American Ice Company. Ice harvesting was big business in the Gardiner area, and in 1909, four years after this photograph was taken, the American Ice Company was convicted and fined for restraining competition and creating a monopoly. The *Kennebec Journal* reported the hearing and quoted Deputy Attorney General John Stanchfield on December 9, 1909, as saying: "Since ice is a necessity of life there should be no monopoly of supply."

The company had also run into trouble in 1907. On June 22, 1907, the Great Falls houses in South Gardiner (which were owned by the company) burned to the ground. The houses sat just north of the South Gardiner Lumber Mill, and the blaze threatened the mill and the north end of the village, but only consumed the Great Falls houses and several surrounding buildings. The *Kennebec Journal* reported the event on June 24, 1907: "The air was filled with an odor which was pleasant to the nostrils and which whetted the appetites of the firemen. It was soon discovered that the odor came from a large hen pen in the rear of one of the burning houses and that a large number of chickens had been roasted alive."

"Ice Harvesting, South Gardiner, Maine," January 20, 1905.

"Thurlow Ice Pond," c. 1900. Farmers cut and stored their own ice from ponds on their land.

"Lawrence Mill, South Gardiner, Maine," November 25, 1902. In 1870, David Lawrence's five grandsons—Sherburn, Samuel, Hiram, Greenleaf, and Charles, Jr.—formed the Lawrence Brothers Lumber Company. The company's original intention was to find a profitable use for the logs that were rejected by the shipbuilding trade but it became the first major industry in South Gardiner (at the peak of its productivity, the company cut 10 million feet of lumber per year) and the leading employer for many years. Local people like Polly remember the Lawrences as paternalistic employers: "If any of the men were sick and couldn't work, Norris Potter's cart was sent and they would fill their larders with groceries."

"View at Bowdoinham, Maine," November 1904. The Lawrence Brothers also operated a mill in Bowdoinham. At this time, the tried and tested, but still extremely dangerous, manual method of moving logs downriver was still used. It required great strength and nerves of steel. South Gardiner resident Roy Bailey recalls the river men: "Andrew Wyman, he was awful religious, Andrew was, a good man. They'd tow them big logs—1,600 logs in a raft—and they'd get down in Merrymeeting Bay and the wind would be blowing awful. They had to make a turn to go up into Bowdoinham [up the Cathance River] and they would swing there a long while before they'd get through. And Andrew, he'd be in the pilot house and he'd say "Blow Jesus! Jesus blow!" and he'd say to Charlie Allen to take the wheel and he'd jump into his boat and start reading the Bible. There was wind there!"

"Lumber Crew and Camp," c. 1910. This photograph shows a camp near the Dead River in the woods. The logs would be cut upriver and sorted for the different mills before they were sent with the river drivers on the treacherous journey downstream. As Roy Bailey remembers: "They all had a mark. I remember Lawrences had one that was cross-w-cross. Before they'd come through this gap, this fellow from South Gardiner—his name was Gross—he'd have on these hob shoes and roll these logs so they could see the mark."

"Piling Logs," August 31, 1909. At the Lawrence Mill logs were piled up on the banks of the river so that when the river froze they could be loaded onto a slip with a crane and moved into the mill.

"Saw Mill in Woods," *c.* 1900. When Kingsbury wrote his *History of Kennebec County* in 1892 the Lawrences employed two hundred men and forty teams for four months of the year and cut eight to nine million feet of logs from their own lands in northern Maine.

"View From Hill," *c.* 1890. The April 24, 1889, edition of the *Gardiner Home Journal* reported that: "The new brick chimney for the Kindlingwood Factory will soon be completed. It is to be one hundred feet high, and will be the largest chimney in New England when finished."

"Mill From Hill," November 1908. A view of Lawrence Mill and the Maine Central Railroad turning house. Bruce Johnson remembers the importance of the railroad in the day-to-day operation of the mill: "The mill had its own spur tracks. Coming up from Richmond, the track went down into Lawrence Mill. The spur portion was owned by the Lawrences. They had a conveyor and loaded [lumber] into the cars that connected into the Maine Central."

"Pulp and Lumber Mills," c. 1900. A view of the Richards Pulp Mill and the South Gardiner Lumber Company taken from the Pittston side of the Kennebec River. South Gardiner resident Wally Atkins has childhood memories of his family's involvement with the lumber industries in South Gardiner: "Mother worked at the Richards Mill, along with Aunt Sade and my grandmother. Many mill employees were women."

"Moulton's Scow," April 4, 1902. Will Moulton, the Crockers, and the Lawrences were prominent in the local scow-building trade. This trade was based at the wharf just below the Lawrence Wharf.

"Scow building: 'Venture'," May 6, 1902. Scows were sloops designed to carry large cargoes in shallower water. A *Kennebec Journal* article announcing the launch of the *Venture* described it as having an 80-horsepower engine, a 45-foot derrick, a 59-foot mast, and a deck surface of 72 by 23 feet.

"Hallowell Quarry," c. 1900. The famous Hallowell granite was quarried from large pits a few miles upriver from Gardiner.

"Shoe Factory, Gardiner," January 17, 1900. This building was erected by the Gardiner Board of Trade in 1896 and in 1898 the Commonwealth Shoe and Leather Company of Whitman, Massachusetts, moved in. By 1949 the company employed 450 men and women who produced 2,700 pairs of "Bostonian" shoes every day.

"Site of New Filter Gardiner, Maine," January 14, 1915. This photograph shows excavation being carried out just below the New Mills bridge as part of the plans for construction of the water filter at the Gardiner Water Works.

"Constructing Filter Gardiner, Maine, Water Works," October 1915. Public works department projects were useful at this time in creating jobs for local people as well as improving vital services.

"Gary Oakes Steers," c. 1900. Well into the twentieth century most rural people tended a family farm with a cow, a few hens, and a vegetable garden, even if they did not farm commercially.

"Canning Factory—Husking," September 26, 1903. A group of mothers and children working in an agricultural factory. Despite the use of some mechanical equipment, agriculture was still very labor intensive in the early twentieth century, and required an "all hands to the deck" attitude. In rural areas children were quite used to working in the fields or on the farm, especially at harvest time, and the school year was designed to accommodate this. With movements to make education more widely available and school attendance compulsory, however, and with increasing concern about child labor, more and more families were required to send their children to school for a certain number of hours each day and a certain number of days each year. The National Parent Teacher Association, founded in 1897, was one organization that was formed largely to respond to the growing public concern over exploitative child labor, especially in mills and factories.

"George Robinson and Team," January 20, 1902. George Robinson lived in the house that stands just north of the present sewer plant in South Gardiner. He would collect grocery orders from customers in rural areas, travel to Gray-Hildreth's wholesalers on Summer Street in Gardiner to pick up the various goods, and then drive around the countryside delivering the groceries. It was a popular service with farming families that lived too far from stores to shop on a regular basis.

"Willey, Cows in Stable," c. 1900. The Willey farm was located on the Capen Road in South Gardiner.

"Viola. lace making," c. 1900. As is true of most societies, women in Victorian America made a valuable contribution to the family and the local economy, both in the home and outside of it. In Maine, we know that women worked alongside the men in the fields and factories, as well as organizing cottage industries such as weaving and lacemaking, running stores and other small businesses, and of course tending to the home and family. Although most histories pay scant attention to this contribution, it is very clear that women often played a key role in keeping a family financed as well as keeping it fed.

"Sheep, Pine Tree Farm," c. 1900. Pine Tree Farm was a sheep farm in Farmingdale. Today the land is used as a golf course.

"McPhee Boy, World War One." Polly has some very personal, very childlike memories of how World War I affected people in South Gardiner: "Leonard Gross . . . he boarded at our house when he enlisted, he and Rodney McPhee. Leonard was really scared . . . One night he came home and sat down in the rocking chair and began to rock back and forth. That old board was squeaking under the chair and he said 'Mrs. Nute, I done it! I done it!' 'Done what Leonard?' she said. 'I enlisted,' he replied." Both Gross and McPhee came home; many did not. W. Clark Noble's memorial to the South Gardiner men who died in the Great War still graces the Congregational Church on Riverview Drive.

"Steam Engine," c. 1900. The turn of the century was a period of great ingenuity in the United States, with many new inventions being developed in what was then still a young and enterprising nation. Bryant had a scientific mind and was fascinated by new inventions and technologies.

Four

The Wider Community

The Kennebec tribe of the Abenaki Native Americans were the first people to inhabit the Kennebec Valley. Their civilization came to an abrupt end with the arrival of European explorers in the seventeenth century, when the disease the explorers carried and the war and famine that resulted from the clash between the two cultures cut the Abenaki population in the region from an estimated three thousand to a mere handful.

By the mid-eighteenth century the lower Kennebec Valley drew new settlers keen to take advantage of its abundant natural resources. Today there are several distinct communities in the Gardiner area: Gardiner, West Gardiner, Farmingdale, Randolph, and Pittston. Connected by river and stream, the towns share a rich history.

In 1849 Gardiner was incorporated as a city, with South Gardiner comprising two thirds of its total territory. Despite periodic friction between the village of South Gardiner and the city proper there has been no serious move to separate. South Gardiner residents have always been proud to be distinct and different, and yet still a part of the city, and this feeling comes through clearly in Bryant's work. He was intimately connected with his neighbors, and yet loved to explore the wider world. He seems to have had a very rare awareness that the images he recorded of life in nineteenth-century South Gardiner were important for posterity as well as for the entertainment of his family, friends, and neighbors. Most of Bryant's images were taken during the industrial heyday of the Gardiner area, so we really get a sense of how vibrant it was at its peak, and how that period affected its history down to the present day.

"Looking Down River From Top of Hill," June 4, 1898. In 1803 the population of Gardiner was 650; by 1880 it was 4,400. After reaching its peak in the industrial era, population growth leveled off, and it has remained fairly constant over the last generation or two. The last census, taken in 1990, figured the population at 6,746.

"Community Hall," c. 1921. The Community Hall was located opposite the Congregational Church on Main Street in South Gardiner. When the Lawrence Mill was torn down in 1920, the lumber and nails were used to build the Community Hall. Local people remember the construction workers carrying lumber up the street from the mill to the building site and straightening the old nails to reuse them, all under the supervision of head carpenter and designer Walter Thurlow.

Wally Atkins remembers the buzz in the village when the building was taking place: "The inside parts that showed were all new lumber. There were dances and minstrel shows. I can remember the opening night. They had a three night affair. They had a stage show—the name of the show was 'The Arizona Cowboy', and the opening line was 'a ringer by the hawk-horn spoon'. When they dedicated the hall, they had a minstrel, a stage show, and I think a big dance." The hall was used by members of every generation—on Saturdays, for instance, the town youth could be found playing basketball in the main hall while the older men played cards in the room out back.

"View In Front of Post Office," *c.* 1900. The South Gardiner Post Office was established in the village in 1870 to serve the many industries there. It was located in various stores and homes—including Forrest Hall, its location in this photograph—before coming to its present location in 1956. Lawrence Mill can be seen on the right.

"Cannard Street Sunday School: Miles Memorial Sunday School," December 25, 1901. The old Baptist church on Cannard Street was replaced with the current South Gardiner Baptist Church located on the River Road. A.N. Weeks testifies to the importance of the church as a community meeting place: "The high points of life depended upon Community-developed pleasures—the Harvest Supper, the Annual Church Fair, the Church Christmas Party with "pieces" spoken, the Drama with local talent and the Sunday school Picnic . . ."

"Church and Parsonage," December 1907.

"Church," December 4, 1908. The South Gardiner Congregational Church was built in 1840 as a "union meeting house" for several protestant denominations. The lumber for construction was donated by the Lawrences. In 1889 the building was raised and a hall built in the lower story. Miss Minnie Bryant always sat in the same pew. When she was invited to sit with a neighbor's family one Sunday, Minnie declined the offer, saying, "My father paid for this pew and I'll not sit anywhere else."

"Crossing From Church Belfry," c. 1900. This photograph, taken from the South Gardiner Congregational Church, shows the Richards Paper Mill in the background. The house in the foreground is today owned by Mrs. Hobart Tracy.

"School," May 9, 1899. A turn-of-the-century school photograph showing Minnie Bryant (third from the right in the top row) and her schoolmates. Polly remembers the kind of discipline used in schools in this period, and how in one instance a female teacher regretted using it: "Miss K . . . her hand was so misshapen. She admitted that day that she went to give T.M. a strapping and she must have had a heavy strap, and he pulled his hand away and it came down on her finger and broke it. She didn't dare to go to the doctor to have it set, afraid he'd ask her how she broke it. She was in agony with it."

"The Lawrence School," c. 1900. The Lawrence family dominated the village of South Gardiner. This photograph shows the Lawrence School at the corner of River and Costello Roads and one of the "Lawrence houses" to the left. Wally Atkins remembers that in the deep Maine winters, area children would be picked up and taken to school on a sleigh.

"School," c. 1930. Free public schools were established in Gardiner in 1784. One hundred years later, there were "districts" of rural primary and "grammar" schools. Scholars who wished to go to high school had to find their own way to Gardiner. Young people were expected to work for their living from a fairly young age, so few stayed on at school past the eighth grade.

"Belgrade," c. 1910. After attending Normal School in Machias, Minnie Bryant taught at Belgrade School. This photograph shows Minnie (third from the left in the top row) and her pupils.

"High Street School Group," c. 1900. Minnie is in the center at the front. A.N. Weeks looks back on the standard of education when he was a boy with a critical eye: "What a strange school! We couldn't choose what we would study! We just studied English, Latin, Ancient History, Algebra and Sciences. If we didn't like it—out! At the end of two years we came to the great crossroad. Either we went on in the college course . . . or we took the business course. . . .What a terrible way to educate children!"

"MacKinley School, West Gardiner," January 14, 1915. Minnie Bryant's father followed her career with his camera. It is interesting to note that in 1860 male teachers were paid $40 per month while their female counterparts earned only $12 per month for performing the same job.

Some of the most menial work in Maine in the nineteenth and early twentieth centuries was done by transients or immigrants. They spoke little English and kept to themselves, often living in makeshift accommodations (such as houseboats on the river in the case of South Gardiner). This anecdote, related by Polly at least eighty years after the event, unfortunately leaves little doubt that most Mainers—except perhaps children—were wary and critical of any outsiders. "They said the 'Dagos' were going to lay the pipes. I kept wondering what 'Dagos' were. So they started the digging and I was all excited—I was going to see a 'Dago'. I saw this ditch with men digging. And I asked where were the 'Dagos'? I couldn't find out why they called them that. I did learn later they were Italians. That's before I knew about those things."

"Laying Water Pipe in South Gardiner," 1914.

"View on the Kennebec, So. Gardiner," *c.* 1900. A.N. Weeks recalls the beauty of the landscape in the Gardiner area in this period: "The four miles from South Gardiner 'up to Gardiner' along the dirt road by the river's edge were leisurely but delightfully accomplished by the good old 'hoss and buggy' method. What bouquets . . . were gathered while Old Nell, with the reins wound around the whip, took her own sweet time on the way home."

"Gardiner Mansion, winter," *c.* 1900. Gardiner's founder, Dr. Sylvester Gardiner, was a stauch Royalist, and during the Revolution he fled to England. His grandson, Robert Hallowell Gardiner, returned to the area after the war to claim his inheritance. The Gothic Revival mansion that he completed *c.* 1836 resembles an English manor house. The Gardiner family has always figured prominently in the economic, cultural, and political life of the entire Kennebec Valley.

"Christ Church Episcopal, Gardiner,"
c. 1900. Robert Hallowell Gardiner
provided substantial financial support for
the construction of this Gothic Revival
church. It was designed by architect
Reverend Samuel Farmer Jarvis and built
of Litchfield granite. It also features a
Paul Revere bell. The church was
consecrated in 1820 and is still in use
today.

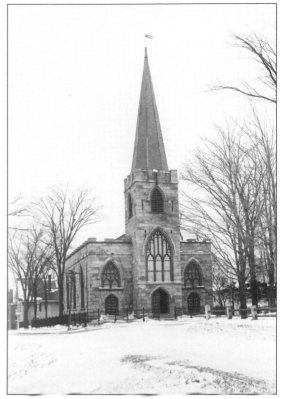

"Fountain," August 6, 1899. Minnie sits
by the Gideon Palmer Memorial
Fountain on the Gardiner Common. The
common is a 5-acre parcel of land that
the Gardiner family donated to the city.
This striking statue of the sea-god Triton
was melted down to make scrap metal
during World War II. It was replaced by a
pile of stones cemented in a pyramid
shape, which made a very poor
centerpiece for the common. The Friends
of Gardiner corrected this by purchasing
and installing the *Woman with Birds*
statue in 1976.

"Arnold Tablet Dedication, Pittston," August 28, 1913.

"Arnold Tablet Dedication, Pittston," August 28, 1913.

"Pittston Chapel" *c.* 1913. This Queen Anne-style church, situated on land donated by Major Reuben Colburn, is very similar in style to the South Gardiner Congregational Church. In 1779 the area on both sides of the river was Pittston. In 1803 Gardiner, on the river's western shore, was set apart. West Gardiner separated from Gardiner in 1850; Farmingdale in 1852.

The Gardiner area has played an important part in American history, including a part in the 1775 Arnold Expedition to Quebec. Major Reuben Colburn was charged by General Washington with providing two hundred bateaux in a short time for an expedition already beset by difficulties and South Gardiner's David Lawrence was among the "Minute Men" who accompanied Arnold.

The Arnold Expedition was a disaster. Contrary to Arnold's belief, there was no true water route to Quebec via the Kennebec. The boats leaked and were heavy to carry over the many long passages of land the men encountered. A remnant of the army did reach Quebec in the dead of winter, and made a heroic attack upon the city. The effort was doomed, but the bravery was not to be forgotten.

In 1913 the Samuel Grant Chapter of the Daughters of the American Revolution erected a tablet to commemorate the 1,100 brave soldiers who marched with Benedict Arnold to Quebec. Three hundred people, the Bryant family among them, gathered at the Major Reuben Colburn House in Pittston (now a museum maintained by the Arnold Expedition Historical Society) for the ceremony. Judge H.S. Webster wrote a poem for the occasion in which he alludes to Arnold's treason:

> We honor them, those men of old,
> Who wrought and fought in Freedom's cause,
> To save for us a land controlled
> By manhood's rights and equal laws...
> And if in some dark hour he err
> From the high vantage of his trust,
> Beneath Ambition's maddening spur,
> Or envy's base, disheartening thrust,
> His recreance our lips will own
> With more of pity than of blame,
> While here, on this memorial stone,
> We dare to blazon Arnold's name.

"Capitol Front: State House, Augusta, Maine," January 23, 1901. Maine's elegant capitol was designed in the Greek Revival style by Charles Bulfinch (1763–1844), architect of the United States Capitol. Completed in 1832, the building was Bulfinch's last major work. In 1889 an addition was made to the back of the building, but Bulfinch's facade was preserved. Herman Bryant photographed the capitol before and after its renovation in 1909.

"State House, Augusta, Maine," c. 1910. In 1909 the capitol was modified following plans drawn up by G. Henri Desmond. It was doubled in size and the dome was raised to a height of 185 feet. The changes ended the controversy over proposals to move the capitol to Portland. The statue gracing the dome is called *Lady Wisdom*. Standing 20 feet high and executed in copper repousse, the statue was South Gardiner native W. Clark Noble's vision of Augusta and the legislative process.

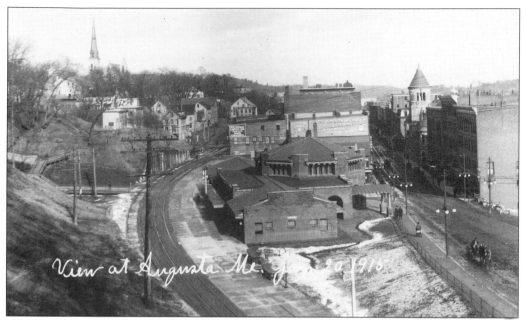

"View at Augusta, Maine," January 20, 1915. The old Augusta train station can be seen in the center.

"Blaine Mansion," January 23, 1901. The Blaine Mansion is shown here at the height of its Victorian splendor. Contrary to popular belief, Blaine never served as governor of Maine. The embellishments he made to the house were an extreme departure from the building's original Federal design. When the house was donated to the state in 1919, eminent Maine architect John Calvin Stevens sought to restore the house to its simple elegance, but he let the cupolas stay.

"Steamer," May 23, 1899. This photograph was taken beside the South Gardiner Congregational Church. In 1885 the fire steamer *City of Gardiner* was brought down from the city proper. Here, it looks ready for the Memorial Day parade.

Herman Bryant was clerk of the South Gardiner Volunteer Fire Department until the month before his death. His neatly sloping hand recorded the activities of the company and the fires they fought, with detailed entries such as this: "27 May 1936 Alarm at 1:15 PM from Box 25 for a chimney fire on Sherburn Avenue in house of Freemont Colpits. Company responded with chemical and booster truck and subdued the fire by the use of the booster line, no damage, time worked 30 minutes. Members all present." In 1932 he was given a silver cup in honor of his many years of service. His last entry, made on June 7, 1937, includes humor that hints at a reluctant realization that he was getting too old to continue: "Records of last meeting read by Second Lieutenant as the Clerk did not have his specs . . ."

A.N. Weeks recalls the basic, but efficient, equipment used by the department: "The ready laid fire in the boiler was ignited by the first to arrive at the engine house and steam would usually be "up" by the time it arrived at the fire . . . Ben Crocker, who used to run the engine used to open it up so wide that the whole mechanism would almost jump up and down on its wheels."

"Fire truck and volunteer fire company, Main Street, S. Gardiner," c. 1931. Shown are, from left to right: (top row) Jerry Casey, Herman Grover, Luther Buckmore, Merton Phillips, Chief Earl Dutton, and Harvey Harlowe; (bottom row) Walter Reynolds, Horace Cox, Eddie Howard, Herman Bryant, and Lawrence Grover.

The Grand Army of the Republic Hall at the bottom of Johnson Street in South Gardiner. Old photographs can sometimes bring memories alive, and this one prompted Wally Atkins to remember some of South Gardiner's characters of old: "Jerome Farrell sold working clothes in the GAR Hall. He lived on Cannard Street. Aunt Sade and his wife had a bakery shop in the parsonage. She and my Uncle Jesse had a store there. Uncle Jesse died in 1903. The way it was told to me he came down with TB. They took his little store and they moved it up into the woods, somewhere up in the back of where Don White's place is now. Him and Aunt Sade went up there to live and that's where he died. After he died, they brought the building back and the hen pen that used to be at Aunt Sade's house was that building."

"GAR Hall Ruins So. Gardiner Maine," November 1911. The GAR Hall hosted many local events, such as this one described in the *Gardiner Home Journal* on January 16, 1889: "The Poverty Ball last week at the new hall was a success in every particular, dress, crowd, music, supper,and financially. W.H. Merrill got the gold piece, two and a half dollars, the prize offered to the one looking the most poverty stricken." The hall burned down in 1911, as A.N. Weeks recalls: "I remember when the GAR Hall burned. At the start there was practically no fire visible—just a small flame in the northwest corner of the outside wall, down at the foundation. This soon became a roaring inferno and the building was a total loss . . ."

Main St. So. Gardiner Me.

"Main Street South Gardiner, Maine from Aunt Annie's Hill," *c.* 1910. Just past the turn to the Capen Road the hill gently slopes into South Gardiner village. The village is much changed today—"automobiles have spoiled it all," said the late Bruce Johnson.

"Snow View Street," *c.* 1900. A view of the River Road in South Gardiner. Once the mills, and therefore the jobs, were gone, South Gardiner's people scattered, and as the number of volunteers available to maintain buildings dwindled, the village's buildings fell into disrepair or burned and were not rebuilt. The "Age of the Individual" exacted a price—the end of an era of community cohesiveness.

Five

A Little Leisure

The Bryant and Thurlow families shared their boat, the *Minnie and Mary*, and a summer cottage at Five Islands. Herman Bryant compiled a poignant pictorial log of time spent with family and friends, and so we have a delightful collection of images of the families loaded in the small motor boat with Herman's camera, tripod, and boxes of glass plates; of the islands and coves along the Kennebec River's route to the sea; of Bath, where Bryant indulged his passion for boats; and of Maine's many tourist spots. Working people had precious little time for leisure and even less money for activities beyond their communities. As both the Bryants and the Thurlows were of moderate means, without their partnership they could not have enjoyed a boat and a cottage on the coast, but the arrangement seems to have worked well. Bryant augmented his income by selling postcards and portraits, but photography was an expensive hobby. Through careful management and hard work the Bryants lived a rich and satisfying life, and made the most of life along the Kennebec.

"Boat at Bowdoinham," *c.* 1910. The Kennebec River was lined with small boat landings, in addition to larger wharves where steamships called.

"Picnic Dinner," *c.* 1905.

"Analdo Taking Picture of the Island, Viola and Minnie," September 10, 1916. Bryant's brother-in-law, Analdo English, was also an amateur photographer. Here he photographs a steamer passing Nahumkeag Island on the Kennebec, near the Bryant home.

"State Fair," c. 1905. This seems to be the Lewiston Fairgrounds, showing the grandstand, the race track, tents, booths, and wagons. Mainers by the thousands still flock to fairs at summer's end to see exhibits, buy treats to eat, and perhaps put a little money on the horses.

"Popham Beach Viola and Minnie," August 15, 1899. Popham Beach, south of Bath at the mouth of the Kennebec River, was as popular with families in the nineteenth century as it is today.

"Wallace Lawrence Horse,"
c. 1900. Wallace Lawrence
(1863–1943) ready for a drive
in the country.

"Stuffed Birds, Willey,"
c. 1900. Hunting and fishing
have always been a staple of
Maine's economy. Many
Mainers used to hunt deer to
eat, but this was sport
hunting.

"Group at Five Islands," *c.* 1900. These fishermen have landed a very large catch. The fish will probably be cooked outdoors later. This is a way of life A.N. Weeks pays tribute to: "What can surpass a fresh-caught shad, not two hours out of the water, when stuffed and baked, lobsters taken from the pots to be boiled in a huge kettle over an open fire on the bank on a summer's eve?"

Minnie and Mary seated on the bow of their namesake during a picnic lunch.

"Yachts at Five Islands," July 1908. The Thurlows, Viola, Frankie, and Minnie with the *Minnie and Mary* at a popular harbor on the east side of Georgetown Island.

"Cottage. . .Five Islands," c. 1908. The Bryants and the Thurlows on the porch of their cottage.

"Fourth of July Group, Five Islands," c. 1908. The Bryants, the Thurlows, and friends after a shore dinner.

The *Minnie and Mary* and a party of women on the rocks at Five Islands.

"Street Wiscasset," c. 1908. When it was built, the Wiscasset bridge was New England's longest—it extended 1 mile and 38 feet across the Sheepscot River. The way Bryant has photographed it makes it appear even longer.

OLD FORT WISCASSET ME.

"Old Fort Wiscasset," July 1908. Fort Edgecomb still stands on Davis Island in the Sheepscot River across from Wiscasset.

"Old Orchard House," *c.* 1903. The Bryants stayed in this hotel on a visit to the world famous Old Orchard Beach.

"Old Orchard From Hotel," *c.* 1903. This photograph, taken from a hotel window, shows the pier and the train station.

"Old Orchard Pier," August 13, 1903. The Saturday evening "Cake Walk" on the pier marquee sounds interesting.

"Orchard Beach," c. 1903. A far cry from the bathing attire seen today at Old Orchard Beach!

"Old Orchard From Pier," August 13, 1903. This was obviously quite a special holiday for the Bryants, as there are many photographs in the collection that were taken here. Perhaps he was trying to create just the right postcard?

"Old Orchard Beach, Maine," c. 1903. This popular Maine resort boasted grand hotels and cottages along the spectacularly beautiful shore.

"Merrymeeting Park Casino," September 13, 1899. Viola and Minnie and two friends posing on the walk.

CASINO MERRYMEETING PARK.

"Casino, Merrymeeting Park," c. 1899. Bryant made a postcard of this view of Merrymeeting Park. The park was built in 1898 on a site 2 miles outside Brunswick. It boasted a zoo and an outdoor dance pavilion, which Bryant also photographed.

"Tent," July 4, 1899. A family snapshot taken by the boardwalk to the Bryant home.

Six

River to the Sea

The Kennebec River engendered vibrant riverfront communities in the eighteenth and nineteenth centuries. Graceful schooners and steamships carried passengers and freight to Boston and beyond. The route became so successful that Cornelius Vanderbilt sent his steamships into competition with a locally owned company in 1838. The Gardiner company responded by chartering the *Huntress* and a fierce race resulted, with the *Huntress* beating the *Vanderbilt* into the Gardiner wharf by an hour. Not to be outdone, Vanderbilt purchased the *Huntress* from the Boston company they had chartered it from and offered it to them for $10,000 more than he paid, with a promise to get out of the Kennebec trade. They accepted.

Even with Vanderbilt gone, competition between the different lines brought price wars. When one line offered free passage to Boston, another countered with free passage plus meals! Races continued and speed began to take precedence over safety. Fights broke out on Gardiner docks between crews of rival ships. The madness ended only after the steamer *Halifax* exploded in Augusta in 1848, killing six passengers.

Fifty years later, Bryant's camera captured an era of commercial and pleasure travel which made living along the Kennebec a joy for a true boat lover

"Boat at Chelsea," *c.* 1910. The *Minnie and Mary* carried the friends up and down the river to the coast and to the islands.

View down the Kennebec River So. Gardiner Me. 1898

"View Down the Hill Showing Vessels," July 9, 1898. The hill behind the Bryant home provided a perfect vantage point for watching the activity on the river. In this photograph log booms line the shore, a three-masted schooner waits at anchor at Goodwin's Point ice house, and a tug tows two more schooners up the river past Nahumkeag Island. The ice house furthest downriver is Haley's in Richmond, which was struck by lightning and burned on May 14, 1900.

"Our Wharf," c. 1900. The *Minnie and Mary* had its home mooring on the Kennebec at the foot of the hill below Phillips Street. In this picture, Viola and Minnie are on the dock and Frankie is in the rowboat.

"Nahumkeag Island," November 1909. This island had many myths told about it. According to an article in the May 22, 1937, edition of the *Kennebec Journal*, the island "is reputed to be one of the places where the pirate Captain Kidd is said to have concealed part of his loot." The Moulton family owns the island—their family home is shown on the Pittston above.

"View From Hill M., M., and F.," August 1907. Minnie, Frankie, and "M" viewing the river at low tide. A tidal river presents unique navigation problems, as anyone who boats on this river knows.

"Breaking Ice on the Kennebec River," December 31, 1901. Ice breakers, like the *Ice King* and the *Knickerbocker* seen here, were useful for towing barges and schooners as well as for preventing ice jams from taking down bridges in the spring thaw. Ice breakers are still sent upriver by the US Coast Guard.

Barges were used in the ice shipping trade as well as in the lumber trade. Occasionally a vessel would be caught by a sudden icing of the river in early winter requiring not only a tow but a metal-hulled tug to break its path.

"Ice Breaking Up, South Gardiner, Maine," c. 1900. Ice going out of the river still heralds spring to those who live along the Kennebec. However, punting in small boats near large moving icebergs is not recommended for amateurs!

"Ice Going Out, South Gardiner, Maine," April 7, 1911. Note what looks like a small windmill behind the house in the center of the photograph.

"High Water," December 16, 1901. The Kennebec River, always full in spring from winter runoff and heavy rains, has flooded its banks on many occasions. Here it covers Main Street by the Lawrence Mill in 1901, the year that the local paper reported that 11 feet of water flowed over the dam at Augusta. Older residents still talk about the terrible 1936 flood, but of more recent memory is the highest recorded flooding in 1987. Potter's Store can be seen behind the rowboat.

"High Water View From Potter's Store," December 16, 1901. This picture appeared in local author Jennie Everson's book, *Tidewater Ice*. She wrote that this ship, the *Leora M. Thurlow* from Bath, was caught by the "freshet" while loading lumber at Lawrence Mills.

Main Street (South Gardner) submerged by the 1936 flood. Bryant's wry sense of humor shows in this photograph, which he has composed so that the sign "Private way, enter at your own risk" can be seen.

"Church Crossing," March 15, 1936. This photograph shows three buildings which are no longer there: a tavern, a dry goods store/gas station, and the post office. Low points of land, particularly those like this by tributary streams, are especially vulnerable to floods.

Another stream flowing into the Kennebec River at the bottom of "Delong's" hill backed up in the 1936 flood. Minnie stands by the fence to give the photograph some scale. Although the river did not get as high in 1936 as it did in 1987, the earlier flood was more destructive due to the damage done by the huge cakes of ice crashing into trees, bridges, and buildings. The house in the center is now the home of the Hart family.

"Dredge at Work, S. Gardiner, Me," c. 1910. When the channels filled with silt and sand and other debris from logs going downriver, dredges cleaned the river bottom to keep it navigable. The sand dredged from the river was dumped on the shore, in places like "the sands," just below the Richmond line. Bruce Johnson remembers that the by-product of this artificial creation was that it created an area where local children could swim.

"Log Boat," October 4, 1901. Log boats were essentially floating hotels for the river men during log drives.

Lawrence Boom So. Gardiner Me.

"Lawrence Boom," November 7, 1909. Log booms were rebuilt each year after winter ice and spring floods.

"Shipping Ice," c. 1900. A.N. Weeks recalls the constant traffic on the river in its heyday: "Schooners came and went all summer, carrying the clear, cold reviver to many parts of the world, sometimes as far away as South America and the Orient."

"Four Master—Weekses," July 4, 1902. Ice harvested during the winter was stored in ice houses awaiting shipment by schooner to markets all over the world. Because they relied on sea winds for their sails, most schooners were towed by tugs to and from the ocean at Merrymeeting Bay.

"Vessel Laying at Anchor Waiting to Load With Ice," September 11, 1898.

"Della Collins," c. 1900. The *Della Collins* was built by the Kennebec and Boston Steamboat Company in 1882 to carry passengers and freight to the cities of Hallowell and Augusta. The fare for a return ticket from Augusta, Hallowell, or Gardiner to Boston was $3, and meals purchased on board cost 50¢. The river men's boat can be seen tied up to the log raft.

"Campground Float," *c.* 1906. The steamer *City of Augusta* passes the dock at the "Richmond Campground," a summer camp for religious revival meetings. Owned by the Eastern Steamship Company, the *City of Augusta* was launched in 1906 to succeed the *Della Collins*. The vessel was described as "odd looking but trim," and it had a crew of twenty under Captain Lewis, who had commanded the *Della Collins* for twenty-five years.

"Islander at Wharf, So. Gardiner, Me," *c.* 1910. According to an advertisement, the *Islander* left the "town" wharf in Gardiner at 7 a.m. every day and carried passengers and freight to Boothbay and the islands, with stops along the way. It returned to Gardiner by evening, and also called at Hallowell and Augusta. A successor *Islander* still plies the coastal waters and docks at Boothbay.

"City of Bangor," July 14, 1914. The *City of Bangor* was owned by the Eastern Steamship Company. Captain Jason Collins recalled that in 1901 the Eastern Steamship Company purchased all the steamers and wharves from the Kennebec Steamboat Company, for the first time transferring ownership out of the Kennebec Valley.

"On the Kennebec River South Gardiner, Maine: "City of Rockland," August 1909. The *City of Rockland* was also owned by the Eastern Steamship Company. In 1922 it was captained by Prescott Taylor. In a history report she prepared for a school project, Minnie Bryant noted that this steamer ran into a rock in heavy fog when it was leaving the Kennebec on a trip to Boston. The ship was so heavily damaged that it was set on fire and destroyed at sea.

"Kennebec," July 4, 1899. The *Kennebec* was built in 1889 and captained by Jason Collins. Here she is heading south past the log floats. Polly remembers that Fourth of July festivities in the Gardiner area were focussed on the river: "Fourth of July was when they did the log rolling contests. We used to get fireworks. They had all kinds of shoots and things and they'd take out the sparklers and let us kids have those."

"Ransom B. Fuller," July 1904. The *Fuller* was owned by the Eastern Steamship Company. She made regular trips to Boston with stops along the way. The vessel was 278 feet long with a galley which ran its length and staterooms for passenger comfort. The railroad eventually put steamships out of business, as trains could travel faster and could operate all year round.

A spectacular view of the old Gardiner wharf, showing the Coliseum and the outlet of the Cobbossee Stream. A 1947 pamphlet from the Gardiner Board of Trade noted: "Old timers were heard to comment that many places one could almost walk across the Kennebec, stepping from ship to ship." The Coliseum was built in 1884, at which time it was the state's largest exhibition hall. It burned in 1903, so we can confidently date this photograph to c. 1900.

"Steam Yacht 'Syrdonia'," August 22, 1911. Bryant was obviously very impressed when he wrote of the *Syrdonia*: "Owned by Cyrus H. K. Curtis of Philadelphia, 176 feet long, draws nine feet of water, carries a crew of 21 men." Curtis, whose career was a real-life "rags to riches" story, owned the publishing house that produced such publications as the *Ladies' Home Journal*, and the *Saturday Evening Post*. Local historian Gary Elwell says Curtis was a "global sensation" when he returned by yacht to present the famous Kotcschmar organ to his native City of Portland.

"Yacht at Gardiner: The Montclare," July 11, 1903. The industrial era made fortunes for entrepreneurs. Here the crew of another private yacht awaits the orders to sail.

Shilo Steamer Baracourta

"Shilo Steamer "Baracourta," October 13, 1916. The *Baracourta* at the Cedar Grove dock of the American Ice Company. Religious cults are not a new social phenomenon: Shiloh was a religious cult based in Durham (near Brunswick). It was begun by Frank W. Sandford, who claimed he was Elijah the Prophet, and required that his followers, or Shilohites, give him all their earthly possessions. The Shiloh community sent out ships such as the vessel shown here to "bring the kingdom" to the far corners of the world, and many followers died of disease and malnutrition both on board the ships and at the community on the hill. At the time this photograph was taken Sandford was serving a sentence for manslaughter, and one can imagine that the sensational trial must have made the arrival of this ship in the Kennebec quite an event. A small Christian "kingdom" congregation still worships weekly at the Shiloh site in Durham. Many among the regular congregation are descendants of the original Shilohites. They no longer sign over their possessions or swear allegiance to the late Sandford.

"Squirrel Island," c. 1900. The *Minnie and Mary* is tied up at the dock of Squirrel Island, just off Southport Island in Boothbay Harbor.

"Doubling Point Light," c. 1900. Built in 1898, this lighthouse at Arrowsic Island (south of Bath) still warns mariners of the sharp bend in the Kennebec River. Today the same view includes the huge cranes of Bath Iron Works on the far shore. Though the lighthouse is now automated, in Bryant's day a keeper would have tended it. The dwellings at the end of the causeway are offices for US Coast Guard personnel.

"Boats and Landing, Capitol Island," *c.* 1900. The *Minnie and Mary* is easy to pick out with her sun canopy on. The party is disembarking for a shore dinner on the pier.

"Westport," *c.* 1900. Aboard the *Minnie and Mary* the two families explored the coastal islands hugging the shore along Merrymeeting and Sheepscot Bays. Today the river is once again full of pleasure boats taking excursions to the sea.

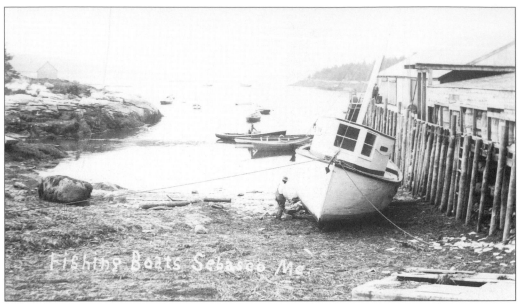

"Fishing Boats, Sebasco, Maine," *c.* 1900. Sebasco is south of Bath on the Phippsburg peninsula.

"School House Malaga Island," *c.* 1910. Malaga Island faces Sebasco on the mainland. The schoolhouse was built in 1908, but just three years later, in 1911, it was the only building not torn down on the island.

FAMILY GROUP MALAGA ISLAND

"Family Group Malaga Island," c. 1910. Reputedly descended from runaway slaves, Malaga's people eked out an existence on a barren, rocky outcropping, no different to poor rural people elsewhere in the state.

The inhabitants of Malaga aroused curiosity and prejudice—they were felt to be an embarrassment to coastal communities seeking to draw tourists and a burden on town welfare rolls. When arguments erupted at the beginning of the twentieth century over whose responsibility the islanders should be, the state was pressured to acquire the island so that its fifty or so inhabitants could be evicted. Some ended up at the state's home for the mentally "feeble" while others literally drifted from shore to shore, their pitiful belongings on makeshift rafts. This particular group of "Mainers" found little welcome as they searched for a home.

In a 1980 *DownEast* article William David Barry described the events at Malaga, the "arbitrary eviction of its population and dismantling of their homes," as a "shameful footnote in Maine history." The island drew photographers who sold postcards of the black inhabitants of Malaga throughout New England. This portrait, however, seems more evocative than exploitative—Bryant made no attempt to photograph the family as anything but a rural Maine family, much the same as any other across the state at this time.

"Four Master, Full Sail," *c.* 1900. In order to photograph this moving ship, Bryant had to control his own boat's speed and its distance from the subject with great accuracy to capture a sharp image. This picture shows his great skill and craftsmanship.

"Five Master," *c.* 1900. A launching, probably at Bath. In his 1935 *History of American Sailing Ships*, Howard Chapell describes the decision to build five- and six-masted ships as an attempt to compete with the early barge lines. The schooners were fast but could be unwieldy. Five-masted ships were built at Bath and at Rockland.

"Iron War Ship Building, Bath, Maine," c. 1900. This is probably the *Monitor* shown below.

"On Board "Monitor," Bath, Maine, Minnie and Viola," August 11, 1900. Bryant was fascinated by ships and enjoyed attending launchings and touring ships such as this one.

"Gunboat Topeka," *c*. 1903.

"On Board Gunboat," *c*. 1903.

"Gun on Gunboat Topeka," August 30, 1903. Bath was a favorite place of Bryant's. His collection is replete with photographs of military ships such as this one. Bath Iron Works still builds ships for the US Navy.

"Boat and Vessel, Wiscasset," c. 1900. This shows the steering wheel and motor in the center of the *Minnie and Mary*. Mr. Thurlow is seated next to his youngest daughter Marjorie, sporting his customary "captain's" hat.

Minnie Bryant's old Ford in front of the parsonage of the South Gardiner Congregational Church, c. 1960. Minnie and her father continued their love of traveling and exploring with this car, but Viola adamantly refused to ride in it. Minnie owned it for many years, and drove it to Bangor, Portland, and Lewiston, but always very slowly. One day a local policeman spoke to her politely, but in great frustration, as she told a neighbor later: "Miss Bryant, there's no law on this earth to tell you how fast you must go—but would you please get going? You're holding up traffic!"

Select Bibliography

Barry, William David. "The Shameful Story of Malaga Island." *DownEast* (November 1980): 53ff.

Bibber, Joyce. *Brunswick and Topsham*. Old Photograph Series (Augusta: Alan Sutton, 1994).

Caldwell, Bill. *Lighthouses of Maine*. (Portland: Gannet Books, 1986).

The Centennial of Gardiner. (Portland: Lakeside Press, June 25, 1903).

Chapelle, Howard I. *The History of American Sailing Ships*. (New York: W.W. Norton and Company, 1935).

Clark, Joanne D., and Leroy A. Congdon. *An Architectural and Historical Survey of The Gardiner Area*. (Gardiner: The Friends of Gardiner, 1984).

Connor, James. *Gardiner: Its History*. (N.p.: James Connor, 1987).

Danforth, William S. "List of Vessels Built in the Vicinity of Gardiner, Maine, 1783–1908." (N.p.: n.d.).

Elwell, Gary F. *By Land; By Sea: Portland Civil War Leader*. (Hallowell: Gary F. Elwell, August 1995).

Erskin, Robert, Lauren M. Sanborn, and Elmer D. Colcord, eds. *The Gardiner Story, 1849–1949*. (N.p.: The City of Gardiner, 1949).

Everson, Jennie G. *Tidewater Ice of the Kennebec*. (Freeport: The Bond Wheelright Company, 1970).

Gardiner, R.H. *Early Recollections 1782–1864*. (Hallowell: White and Horne Company, 1936).

Hanson, John W. *History of Gardiner, Pittston, and West Gardiner*. (Gardiner: n.p., 1852).

Harding, R. Brewster. *Greetings From Maine*. (Portland: Old Port Publishing Company, 1975).

Hunt, Draper H., and Gregory Clancy. *The Blaine House, Guide and Brief History*. (N.p.: Maine Historic Preservation Commission, 1983).

Kershaw, Gordon E. *The Kennebec Proprietors 1749–1775*. (Portland: Maine Historical Society, 1975).

Kingsbury, H. *Illustrated History of Kennebec County*. Bk. 3 (New York: H.W. Blake and Company, 1892).

Lemar, Frank. "History of Gardiner Fire Department 1850–1937." (N.p.: July 24, 1937).

Maine Old Cemetery Association. *Maine Cemetery Inscriptions*. Bks. 3 and 4 (N.p.: Maine State Library, n.d.).

Marriner, Ernest. *Kennebec Yesterdays*. (Waterville: Colby College Press, 1954).

Nelson, Shirley. *Fair Clear and Terrible*. (Latham: British American Publishing, 1989).

Newhall, Beaumont. *The History Of Photography*. (New York: The Museum of Modern Art, 1964).

Patterson, Louise Ware. *Vignettes of Gardiner*. (Hallowell: Louise Ware Patterson, n.d.).

Randall, Willard Sterne. *Benedict Arnold: Patriot and Traitor*. (New York: Morrow, 1990).

Shettleworth, Earle E. Jr., and Frank A. Beard. *Maine State House*. (N.p.: Maine Historic Preservation Commission, 1981).

Smith, Danny D., with Joanne D. Clark. *Gardiner's Yellow House: A Tribute to the Richards Family*. (Gardiner: The Friends of Gardiner, 1988).

Smith, Justin H. *Arnold's March From Cambridge to Quebec*. (New York: G.P. Putnam's Sons, 1903).

Stover, Mirriam Thomas. *Flotsam and Jetsam*. (N.p.: Mirriam Thomas Stover, 1973).

Varney, George J. *Varney's Gazetteer of Maine*. (N.p.: 1882).

Webster, Henry Sewall, ed. *Gardiner, Maine Vital Records to 1892*. (Boston: Stanhope Press, 1915).

Weeks, Arnold Noble. *Memoirs*. (N.p.: n.d.).

Zimmet, Abby. "A Stone's Throw From Civilization, Malaga Island Bore Legacy of Neglect." *Maine Sunday Telegram* (January 1, 1995).